EDGE BOOKS

STARS OF PRO WRESTLING

RANDY ORTON

By Jason D. Nemeth

Consultant:
Mike Johnson, Writer
PWInsider.com

Capstone press

Mankato, Minnesota

Edge Books are published by Capstone Press,
151 Good Counsel Drive, P.O. Box 669, Mankato, Minnesota 56002.
www.capstonepub.com
Printed in the United States of America in Stevens Point, Wisconsin.
042011
006150R

Library of Congress Cataloging-in-Publication Data
Nemeth, Jason D.
    Randy Orton / by Jason D. Nemeth.
    p. cm. — (Edge. Stars of pro wrestling.)
    Includes bibliographical references and index.
    Summary: "Describes the life and career of pro wrestler Randy Orton"
— Provided by publisher.
    ISBN 978-1-4296-3348-2 (library binding)
    1. Orton, Randy. 2. Wrestlers — United States — Biography — Juvenile
literature. I. Title. II. Series.
GV1196.C67N47 2010
796.812092 — dc22
[B]   2009002180

Editorial Credits
Mandy Robbins, editor; Ted Williams, designer; Jo Miller, media researcher

Photo Credits
DEFENSEIMAGERY/SSGT Richard P. Tudor, USMC, 11
Getty Images Inc./WireImage/Djamilla Rosa Cochran, 15; Don Arnold,
    cover, 12; Kevin Mazur, 17, 18
Globe Photos/Allstar/Graham Whitby-Boot, 26
Landov LLC/Alpha, 24
Newscom, 10; Splash News and Pictures/Heather Rousseau, 23; WENN/
    Carrie Devorah, 19, 21, 28
Shutterstock/George Koroneos, 9; Lori Martin, 5
Zuma Press/Icon SMI/Tom 'Mo' Moschella, 6, 22

Design Elements
Shutterstock/amlet; Henning Janos; J. Danny; kzww

TABLE OF CONTENTS

Chapter 1

MAN OF DESTINY

Randy Orton strutted into the arena at SummerSlam 2004. The 24-year-old jumped into the ring, climbed the ropes, and posed for the crowds. "It's Randy Orton's destiny," said the announcer, "to be the youngest world champion in the history of WWE."

Current champion Chris Benoit entered the ring carrying the championship belt. The two men faced off. Minutes into the fight, Randy used Benoit's **signature move**, the *sharpshooter*, against him. Benoit struggled, but he eventually escaped.

The fight went back and forth. At one point, Randy ended up outside the ring. Benoit dove out of the ring to hit him. Randy dodged. Benoit hit the wall and hurt his neck. Randy then performed a *neck-breaker* on Benoit. This move wore down the champion.

signature move — **the move for which a wrestler is best known**

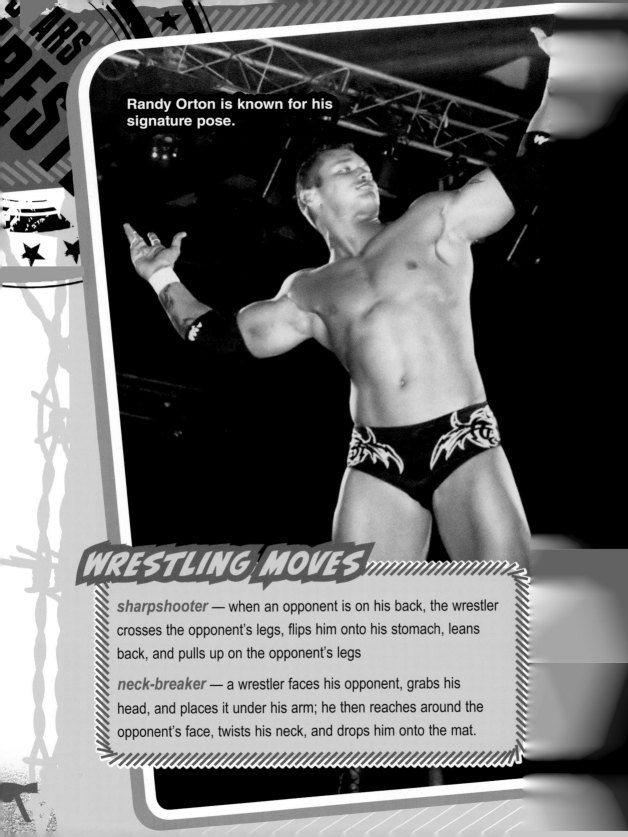

Randy Orton is known for his signature pose.

WRESTLING MOVES

sharpshooter — when an opponent is on his back, the wrestler crosses the opponent's legs, flips him onto his stomach, leans back, and pulls up on the opponent's legs

neck-breaker — a wrestler faces his opponent, grabs his head, and places it under his arm; he then reaches around the opponent's face, twists his neck, and drops him onto the mat.

Benoit won the championship title at WrestleMania in March 2004.

DESTINY IN QUESTION

Benoit made a comeback near the end of the match. He put Randy in the sharpshooter. Randy almost passed out from the pain. The referee lifted Randy's arm and let it go. It dropped to the mat. The referee dropped his arm a second time. Randy would lose if it dropped a third time. But he regained his strength and grabbed the bottom rope. Benoit had to break his hold.

Benoit then gave Randy a *German suplex*, slamming Randy's head and back into the mat. Benoit did this six times in a row. Randy lay flat in the middle of the ring. Perhaps the championship was not his destiny after all.

WRESTLING MOVES

German suplex — standing behind his opponent, a wrestler wraps his arms around his waist; he then lifts him over his shoulder and falls backwards, driving the opponent's head and shoulders into the mat.

Chapter 2

THIRD-GENERATION WRESTLER

Randy Orton was born April 1, 1980, in Knoxville, Tennessee, to Elaine and Bob Orton Jr. According to Randy, being born into a wrestling family was the best thing that happened for his career. His grandfather, Bob Orton Sr., wrestled in the 1950s and 1960s. His father wrestled in the 1970s and 1980s. His uncle Barry wrestled too. Randy is one of very few third-generation wrestlers.

When Randy was a boy, many of his father's wrestling friends visited his home. He met "Rowdy" Roddy Piper, Mr. Fuji, and Greg "The Hammer" Valentine. One time, Andre the Giant leaned on the Ortons' banister and broke it!

Randy dreamed of becoming a professional wrestler from a young age.

TO WRESTLE OR NOT TO WRESTLE

As a kid, Randy wanted to grow up to join the family business. He wrestled in an **amateur** league as a child. Later on, Randy wrestled for Hazelwood Central High School. Randy made it all the way to the Danny Hodge World High School Championships.

But life as a professional wrestler can be tough. Wrestlers spend a lot of time away from their families. Randy's mom and dad wanted him to do something different.

amateur — describes a sports league that athletes take part in for pleasure rather than for money

In the Marines, soldiers learn to handle an M16 rifle.

Randy spent 38 days in military jail at Camp Pendleton when he was dishonorably discharged from the Marines.

Randy took their advice. When he graduated from high school, Randy joined the United States Marine Corps. Randy only spent one year in the Marines. He went **AWOL** twice and disobeyed a direct order. This led to his dishonorable discharge. According to Randy, he got discharged on purpose. He wanted to start his wrestling career.

AWOL — leaving one's military duties without permission; stands for "absent without leave."

GETTING STARTED

In 2000, Randy signed a developmental contract with World Wrestling Entertainment (WWE). He trained for two years with Ohio Valley Wrestling (OVW). Randy won the OVW Hardcore Championship title twice.

On April 25, 2002, Randy made his WWE television debut against Hardcore Holly. Randy was only 22 years old. He won his first match. A few weeks later, Randy was sidelined with foot and shoulder injuries. He couldn't wrestle for a few months.

Pro Wrestling Illustrated named Randy the 2001 Rookie of the Year.

Orton Family Legacy

The Orton family legacy began with Bob Orton Sr. Born in 1929, "The Big O" made his wrestling debut in 1951. Orton Sr. would also be known as Rocky Fitzpatrick, El Lobo, and Zodiak.

Both of Orton's sons followed in his footsteps. Bob Orton Jr. was born in 1950. He made his wrestling debut in 1972. Fans knew him as Cowboy Bob Orton. Cowboy Bob sported his signature cowboy hat. He also wore a cast on his arm for many years that doubled as a weapon.

Barry Orton was born in 1958. While his real passion was for music and movies, Barry also fell into the family business. He made his debut in 1976. Barry went by the names Superstar Barry O and his father's former nickname, Zodiak.

WRESTLING FACT

The Orton family has held 11 championship titles. Randy won five of them.

Chapter 3

THE LEGEND KILLER

By May 2003, Randy was back in the ring. He formed a group called Evolution with Batista, Triple H, and Ric Flair. Randy learned a lot from these experienced wrestlers. Evolution was a **heel** group. The group **feuded** with many other wrestlers. According to Randy, Evolution was the second-best thing for his career.

ATTACKING LEGENDS

In 2003, Randy started calling himself the Legend Killer. He vowed to defeat every legendary wrestler in WWE. At Unforgiven 2003, Randy wrestled Shawn Michaels. Randy used a pair of brass knuckles to knock out Michaels. The Legend Killer had become a reality.

heel — a wrestler who acts like a villain in the ring
feud — to take part in a long-running quarrel

Randy beat on Mick Foley at
WrestleMania in 2004, while his
Evolution teammate Batista stood by.

Randy soon faced Sergeant Slaughter. Sergeant Slaughter had wrestled Randy's father and grandfather. At the end of a tough match, Randy finally beat the Sergeant with an *RKO*.

HARDCORE LEGEND

In 2004, Randy started a feud with Mick Foley. The feud led to a Hardcore match at Backlash 2004. Foley was known as the Hardcore Legend.

The mat was covered in thumbtacks, and weapons were allowed. One weapon was a bat covered in barbed wire. The wrestlers could also use metal garbage cans. Both men fought until they were bloody. At one point, Foley slammed Randy into the mat. When Randy got up, thumbtacks were sticking into his back. Randy recovered, though, and won by using his RKO. He dropped Foley onto the barbed wire baseball bat for the pin.

WRESTLING MOVE

RKO — stands for "Randall Keith Orton;" a wrestler stands to the side and slightly in front of his opponent, wraps his arm around his opponent's neck, and drops to the ground.

Randy pinned Mick Foley at WrestleMania.

During his time in Evolution, Randy was not just going after legends. He was also going after gold. At Armageddon 2003, Randy defeated Rob Van Dam to win the Intercontinental Championship. The Intercontinental belt was Randy's first WWE championship, but it wouldn't be his last.

WRESTLING FACT

Randy is one of only a few other third-generation wrestlers in WWE. Others include The Rock, Ted DiBiase Jr., and Chavo Guerrero.

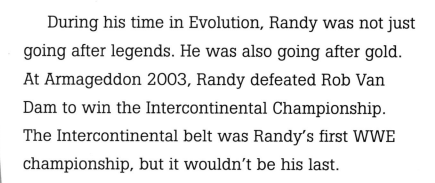

The Intercontinental Championship was the first of many titles Randy would win.

Legends Killed: R.I.P.

* The Fabulous Moolah, September 15, 2003
* Shawn Michaels, September 21, 2003
* "Stone Cold" Steve Austin, November 16, 2003
* Sergeant Slaughter, November 24, 2003
* Rob Van Dam, December 14, 2003
* Mick Foley, April 18, 2004
* Ric Flair, October 19, 2004
* Jake "the Snake" Roberts, March 14, 2005
* Undertaker, August 21, 2005
* "Rowdy" Roddy Piper, October 3, 2005
* Tommy Dreamer, May 29, 2007
* "The American Dream" Dusty Rhodes, July 22, 2007

Shawn Michaels was one of the first legends Randy took down.

Chapter 4

CHASING LEGENDS AND GOLD

The next title Randy went after was the World Heavyweight Championship belt. Randy claimed it was his destiny to become the youngest World Heavyweight Champion in WWE history. He got the chance to prove it at SummerSlam 2004.

But as the match against Chris Benoit went on, it looked like Randy's destiny was in question. When Randy looked ready to give up, Benoit climbed to the top rope. He dove onto Randy to finish him. Suddenly, Randy lifted his legs. Benoit's face smashed into Randy's boots, and he fell to the mat. Randy tried for the pin, but Benoit kicked out. It wasn't over yet.

Randy spends 12 hours a year "under the needle" to keep his many tattoos looking fresh.

Benoit put Randy in a *crossface*, but Randy rolled out of it. He surprised the crowd by suddenly performing his signature RKO on Benoit. Randy grabbed Benoit's head, leapt into the air, and dropped him face-first onto the mat. Benoit was out cold. Randy Orton's destiny was fulfilled.

WRESTLING MOVE

crossface — when the opponent is on his stomach, the wrestler reaches around his head with both arms, locks his hands together, and pulls back on the opponent's neck

Randy defeated Chris Benoit and his high-flying wrestling style.

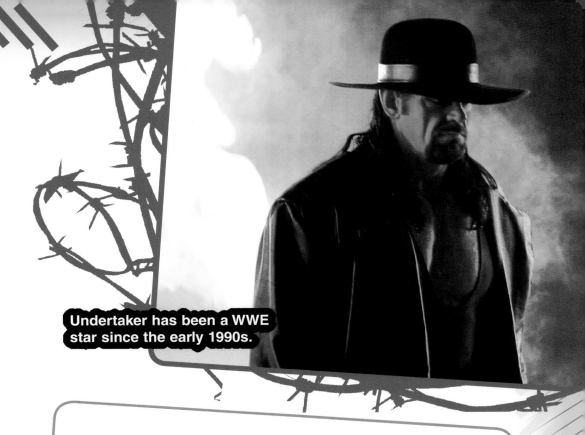

Undertaker has been a WWE star since the early 1990s.

TAKING ON UNDERTAKER

In 2005, Randy took on Undertaker. Undertaker had never lost a match at WrestleMania. Randy challenged him to a match at WrestleMania that year. Randy lost, but he wasn't discouraged.

Cowboy Bob Orton came back to WWE later that year. Together, the father and son feuded with Undertaker. At No Mercy 2005, the two Ortons beat Undertaker in a Handicap Casket Match. They stuffed him into a coffin for the win. Then they poured gasoline on top of the coffin and lit it on fire.

Terry Bollea began wrestling in 1978 as Sterling Golden. He later changed his ring name to Hulk Hogan.

FACING THE HULK

Beating Undertaker wasn't enough for Randy. After that feud ended, he challenged the biggest WWE legend of all.

In 2006, Randy started feuding with Hulk Hogan. After two months of insults, they settled their dispute at SummerSlam 2006.

When the match began, the crowd went wild for Hogan. Hogan easily overpowered Randy and threw him into the corner. But Randy attacked Hogan's bad knee and slowed him down.

Randy used an RKO to pin Hogan. But the referee noticed Hogan's foot on the bottom rope. The pin didn't count, and the match went on. Hogan dropped Randy with a boot to his face. Then Hogan hit him with a *leg drop* and pinned Randy. Hogan was a legend who wouldn't die.

WRESTLING MOVE

leg drop — a wrestler jumps into the air and lands with his thigh on the opponent's head or chest

Triple H went from being Randy's partner in Evolution to being his opponent.

THE AGE OF ORTON

In October 2007, Randy was scheduled to wrestle John Cena for the WWE Championship. But Cena was injured and couldn't wrestle. WWE owner Vince McMahon gave Randy the belt. Suddenly, Triple H came into the ring and challenged Randy. Randy didn't want to wrestle Triple H. He had already lost his World Heavyweight Title to him. But McMahon was the boss, and he ordered the match to begin.

The fight was intense. Triple H almost got the pin after a couple of powerful *clotheslines*. Randy performed a *DDT* and almost pinned Triple H. In the end, Randy missed a tackle and accidentally hit the ring post. It knocked him out. Randy lost the belt. But the night wasn't over.

Randy demanded a rematch. McMahon agreed. Randy and Triple H met for the second time in one night for a Last Man Standing match. One of the men had to fall for the count of 10 for the other to win. The match was brutal. In the end, Randy defeated Triple H with an RKO onto a table. Randy won the WWE Championship two times in the same night.

He held the title for seven months before losing it again to Triple H. Before he could win it back, Randy broke his collarbone at One Night Stand in 2008.

WRESTLING MOVES

clothesline — a wrestler runs toward the opponent with his arm outstretched and smashes his arm into the opponent's neck

DDT — a wrestler puts his opponent in a front face lock and then falls to the mat, driving his opponent's head into the mat

Randy won the Royal Rumble in January 2009.

Randy was supposed to be out for three months. But then he had a motorcycle accident and broke his collarbone again. The injury kept him out of wrestling for another three months.

Randy was upset to be out of the ring for so long, but the time off couldn't have come at a better time. While he was recovering, his wife, Samantha, gave birth to a daughter. Randy was grateful to be home with his wife and new daughter, Alana.

BACK IN THE RING

On November 3, 2008, Randy finally made his comeback. He lost to CM Punk at his first match back but pinned Batista at Survivor Series later that month. By December Randy had formed a new group called Legacy with Cody Rhodes and Ted DiBiase Jr.

While Legacy is Randy's new group, his legacy will always be that of the Legend Killer. He will have to fight to defend this title. That means facing many more legends and many more championship matches. But wrestling runs in Randy's family. It is in his blood. You could say it's his destiny.

GLOSSARY ★ ★ ★ ★ ★ ★

amateur (AM-uh-chur) — describes a sports league that athletes take part in for pleasure rather than for money

AWOL (AY-wahl) — to leave one's military duties without permission

developmental contract (duh-VEHL-up-ment-tuhl KAHN-tract) — a deal in which a wrestler is paid to compete in a smaller league as a way to train for a bigger league like WWE

dishonorable discharge (diss-ON-ur-uh-buhl DISS-charj) — being kicked out of the military for a serious offense

feud (FYOOD) — to take part in a long-running quarrel between two people or groups of people

heel (HEEL) — a wrestler who acts like a villain in the ring

signature move (SIG-nuh-chur MOOV) — the move for which a wrestler is best known; this move is also called a finishing move.

READ MORE

Kaelberer, Angie Peterson. *Hulk Hogan: Pro Wrestler Terry Bollea.* Pro Wrestlers. Mankato, Minn.: Capstone Press, 2004.

Kaelberer, Angie Peterson. *The Nature Boy: Pro Wrestler Ric Flair.* Pro Wrestlers. Mankato, Minn.: Capstone Press, 2004.

Shields, Brian, and Kevin Sullivan. *WWE Encyclopedia.* New York: DK Publishing, 2009.

INTERNET SITES

FactHound offers a safe, fun way to find Internet sites related to this book. All of the sites on FactHound have been researched by our staff.

Here's all you do:

Visit *www.facthound.com*

FactHound will fetch the best sites for you!

INDEX ★ ★ ★ ★ ★ ★ ★